1 1 AUG ....

KU-542-916

BIS

Please renew or return items by the date
shown on your receipt

www.hertfordshire.gov.uk/libraries

Renewals and enquiries: 0300 123 4049

Textphone for hearing or 0300 123 4041
speech impaired users:

Hertfordshire

L32 11.16

528 700 67 8

ALMA JUNIOR
an imprint of

ALMA BOOKS LTD
3 Castle Yard
Richmond
Surrey TW10 6TF
United Kingdom
www.almajunior.com

Space on Earth first published by Alma Books Ltd in 2019

© Sheila Kanani, 2019

Cover and inside illustrations © Del Thorpe, 2019

Printed in Great Britain by CPI Group (UK) Ltd, Croydon CR0 4YY

ISBN: 978-1-84688-455-9

All rights reserved. No part of this publication may be reproduced, stored
in or introduced into a retrieval system, or transmitted, in any form or
by any means (electronic, mechanical, photocopying, recording or otherwise), without the prior written permission of the publisher. This book is
sold subject to the condition that it shall not be resold, lent, hired out or
otherwise circulated without the express prior consent of the publisher.

CONTENTS

Technology

Health

Fashion

SPACE ON EARTH

Have you ever looked up into the sky and wondered about space, astronomy and the universe? I bet you have. But perhaps you've never looked around you, at the sunglasses you're wearing or the technology you're using, and thought about space? The truth is there is more of space on Earth than you realise!

I've been interested in astronomy since I was thirteen years old, when I saw the film *Apollo 13*. This prompted me to learn more about astronauts, physics and astronomy. In my "space career" I often get asked the question: "Why should we spend money on space when we need the money on Earth?"

The truth is that, even though planetary missions can cost billions of pounds, we *don't* actually spend as much money on the space industry as people might think, and the space industry (including the British one) creates thousands of jobs and brings in a lot of money each year.

It is also important to think about what the space industry provides for us – apart from the obvious! Space is awe-inspiring and exciting, and can be the hook that gets a young person into science. In addition to this, there are hundreds of inventions and technologies created for the space industry that we can benefit from here on Earth.

Space agencies such as the National Aeronautics and Space Administration – or NASA, as it's commonly known – sign agreements promising that the research and innovation created by space agencies should benefit everyone, not just astronauts. And since the space age began, space technology has done just that! In the last sixty years, by partnering with research companies, space agencies have discovered, invented or improved all types of things – from cochlear implants to skiwear – that have enriched our daily lives and, in some cases, saved the lives of humans on Earth. Read on to discover how much of space there really is on Earth!

TECHNOLOGY

Selfies and Pill Cameras

We've probably all taken photos while on holiday or enjoying an adventure with friends. And I'm sure that many of us have turned the camera round to take pictures of ourselves! This is called "taking a selfie", as you know, and the cameras and video equipment on smartphones help us do this.

But the technology in smartphones and cameras isn't just for taking selfies or strapping cameras to your head to video yourself having fun. These tiny cameras have also been developed into pill-sized sensors that can be used in medical procedures. Patients swallow the pill camera so doctors are able to see the inside of the

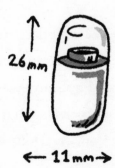

stomach in a safe way. The cameras can also be used for surveillance (spy stuff!) and in the automotive (car) industry.

However, clearly the most popular use for this technology has been in smartphone cameras and taking silly pictures of yourself and your friends...

But did you realise that every time you take a selfie you are using technology that was first designed for the space industry? Imagine – if we didn't have the space industry, we might not have selfies...

AMAZING FACT

The concept of digital photography was actually developed at the NASA Jet Propulsion Laboratory by engineer Eugene Lally in the 1960s, so digital photography *and* selfies are all creations of the space industry!

But how are selfies connected to space?

Smartphone cameras, and others, use a particular type of image sensor called a CMOS (complementary metal-oxide semiconductor), which was created by Eric Fossum, a NASA scientist. Eric used to work on developing new techniques for image-sensing, using smaller and lighter machinery – qualities that are important in the space industry.

Previously, many image sensors used CCD (charge-coupled device) technology to create high-quality digital photographs. These are made from a set of special sections of light on a screen, called pixels, which collect electrical charges when light is shone on them. These charges can be measured and turned into a picture.

The problem with CCDs is that they require lots of power. So NASA hired Fossum to develop CCD imaging sensors into something better. Fossum was able to combine some of the good properties of the CCD into the CMOS, resulting in a sensor that produced clearer images. CMOS pixels read their own signals, instead of collecting and transferring charges like CCDs, meaning they use less energy and are more efficient. An added benefit was that almost all the other camera electronics could then be put into the computer chip with the CMOS, developing more compact, reliable and cheaper computer-chip-sized cameras that could be used in smartphones and digital video equipment.

AMAZING FACT

When Eric Fossum first came up with the idea for this technology, many people, including his friends, didn't take him seriously! He had to push for companies to use his CMOS sensors and chip-sized cameras, and it took almost ten years for his invention to be used more widely.

MEET THE SCIENTIST

Eric Fossum was born in 1957 and raised in Simsbury, Connecticut. After spending many Saturdays at a science centre – which he says prompted his passion for science – he attended Trinity College and Yale University. In 2017 he won engineering's biggest prize – the Queen Elizabeth Prize for Engineering.

Satellite TV

What is your favourite programme on TV? What channel does it normally come on? The chances are you are watching television that has been sent all over the world, and even into space! This is called satellite television – and many people who have a television will be using it on a daily basis.

Satellite TV delivers programmes to viewers all over the world by relaying TV signals from satel-

lites in orbit around the Earth directly into people's homes. Even if your TV doesn't use a satellite dish, many live transmissions from all over the world depend on satellite technology. Signals from space are received by a satellite dish, usually located on the roof of your home, decoded by your set-top box and transmitted into your TV for your viewing pleasure.

These satellites hover in "geostationary orbit" at about 37,000 km above the Equator. At this distance, the satellites orbit the Earth at the same speed as the Earth rotates, so the satellites appear to stay above the same place on Earth. This is useful, because the dishes on Earth can always be pointed in the same direction towards the satellites in the sky – and they don't need to be readjusted in order to communicate with each other.

This ring of communication satellites covers the whole globe, meaning that a TV signal can be transmitted from the ground up to one of these satellites, and the signal is then amplified and retransmitted by the satellite to another place on Earth. In this way we are able to watch TV from almost anywhere in the world.

Satellite technology is not just for pleasure, though. It is a really useful tool in offices, for scientists and for doctors communicating between hospitals across the globe, from big cities to rural villages. Satellite communication, including radio broadcast, can be used in cars and aeroplanes, and for connecting people all over the globe.

Did you know that television as we know it wouldn't be the same without the space industry?

The use of satellites for communication was developed by the space industry, and over time was used commercially for satellite television. But TV wasn't the primary reason satellite communication was developed: it was first used to allow spacecraft to keep in touch with scientists on Earth.

In July 1962, the experimental satellite Telstar 1 sent the first live TV programme from the USA to the UK, and by 1965 there were regular broadcasts using the first commercial communication satellite, Intel 1, or "Early Bird".

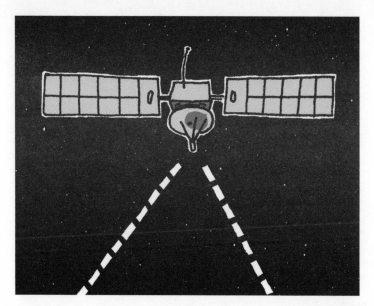

To begin with, the signal had to be sent via a large dish on the Earth before the programmes reached household television screens, but over time technology improved, and now the signal can be sent directly from space to the small satellite dish on your roof.

Special cameras and audio equipment were also developed to record the first man on the Moon, and NASA has had dedicated TV channels since the 1980s.

Nowadays we take it for granted that we can watch international sporting or music events at the touch of a button. These programmes come from all over the world, but it wouldn't be possible if it wasn't for spin-off technology from the space industry.

AMAZING FACTS

After the Apollo 11 mission in 1969, all the special cameras and audio equipment that were designed for it at great expense were left behind on the Moon!

There are over 4,000 satellites dotted around the Earth for the purpose of communication, but only half are currently active.

MEET THE SCIENTIST

Arthur C. Clarke, a famous British science-fiction author, was the first person to come up with the idea of satellite communication – in 1945! He imagined a situation in which three satellites, evenly spaced around the Earth, would help global communication. He won the Franklin Institute's Stuart Ballantine Medal for this in 1963.

Satellite Navigation

Once upon a time, not that long ago, if you wanted to drive a car from one location to another, you would have had to use a road atlas to help you navigate. You would have had to plan your route and the time it might take to get to your destination, step by step, because live traffic information would not have been available. If you took a wrong turn, you would have had to go back to the road atlas to recalculate your route, and it wasn't easy reading a book while trying to drive – especially if you didn't know the area you were travelling to very well!

Nowadays life is much simpler with satnav systems. You enter your destination, and the satnav – short for "satellite navigation" – can work out the best route based on your starting point – and at the touch of a button you're given excellent directions, traffic information, journey length and alternative routes. The satnav can talk to you, so you don't even have to look at the screen, and if you take an incorrect turning, it will recalculate your route and your arrival time. Some satnav systems can also communicate with the people at your destination, so they can tell your friends and family when you're due to arrive at their house.

Satnav technology can be found in many household devices these days, the most obvious being a smartphone. The details of the most popular or useful attractions are usually listed within a satnav system – for example, hotels and restaurants – so that you can search for them with ease. Satnavs are also used for fun outdoor sports like hiking, sailing and cycling.

Satellite navigation has changed the way we are able to navigate – meaning it is now virtually impossible to get lost!

Without space technology, satnavs would be useless.

Satnavs rely on space technology – they need at least four satellites in space, which send out signals and work together with a receiver to determine where you are and the best route to where you are going. A system of satellites is used to give exact positioning and calculate the best routes by first receiving information on where you are located.

Satnavs work by receiving radio signals from satellites orbiting the Earth. There are over thirty satellites for the Global Positioning System (GPS) alone, and the receivers get information from 6–12 satellites at the same time. Each satellite also has a highly specialised clock in it, called an atomic clock, which tells the time precisely at your location.

The original system was created by the US military in the 1960s, and twenty-three satellites were launched to help the USA navigate submarines. Eventually these American satellites grew into the above-mentioned system called GPS, and by the

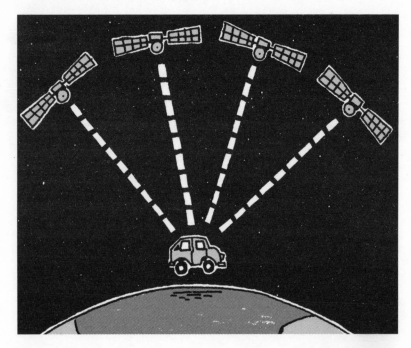

1980s Ronald Reagan, then President of the USA, allowed the system to be used by civilians too. Although satellite navigation was first created for military use, it has a lot of applications in the space industry, and was improved upon greatly by NASA in the 1990s. NASA was able to correct many errors in the GPS system, and continues to monitor it on a daily basis. Many smartphones use the corrected GPS data that NASA developed to get navigation information without the need of an Internet connection.

Satellite navigation has become useful for more than just helping your parents drive their car or you to find your way to a friend's house with your smartphone. GPS can be used to track weather, watch crop production, find out more about climate change, discover how wildfires spread and watch boundaries change. It can detect how the Earth's crust changes after an earthquake, and can monitor the Earth's atmosphere. At NASA, GPS is crucial for helping to understand, protect and monitor Earth.

GPS is not perfectly accurate in its current state – it can locate someone to within 15–20 m, but NASA is working with engineers and scientists to create a "Global Differential GPS" which might be able to locate people within 10–20 cm and work at extremely high latitudes (at locations in the far north or south of the Earth), meaning that people in Greenland and Antarctica could finally get coverage...

AMAZING FACT

NASA scientists are discussing the possibility of creating a satnav system around Mars to enable future astronauts to navigate themselves around the red planet!

Drills and Dustbusters

Have you ever used one of those mini vacuum cleaners called "Dustbusters" to remove any evidence of crumbs from the sofa? Or has your mum or dad ever used an electric drill to put together some furniture or hang a picture on the wall? Chances are you've come across some cordless tools that were made possible by the space industry.

What have drills got to do with space?

Although cordless tools were not initially invented for the space industry, they were later developed in a particular way to enable the Apollo astronauts to complete their jobs on the surface of the Moon. NASA teamed up with Black & Decker in the

1960s, when the company was developing cordless power tools to help those who were installing windows from the outside of houses.

NASA realised that cordless technology would be extremely useful in space, where plug sockets are hard to come by! So they worked with Black & Decker to make a spanner that could drill bolts into place in microgravity (when the forces of gravity are very weak but not quite absent) without causing the astronaut to spin... A cordless rotary drill was also created specifically for the Apollo astronauts when they were on the Moon. The drill was for extracting rock samples from the surface, and was designed to work in the extreme conditions found in space, such as cold temperatures and the absence of atmosphere.

The lunar drill had to be lightweight and compact, but it also had to do its job really well. The lunar surface was hard and the drill had to bore a hole up to three metres deep! Although the drill could have used power from the Lunar Module, the drilling locations were often too far from the base station, so it needed to be cordless.

To make the drill more effective, Black & Decker created computer programmes to make it work properly. These programmes were then used in subsequent technology development, but Black & Decker wouldn't have created them if it hadn't been for NASA.

The spanner and the drill had to be tested before they were flown into space, and Black & Decker, with guidance from NASA, ran trials underwater and in a "vomit comet" – an aeroplane designed to fly at high altitudes and then dive down almost immediately – in order to simulate microgravity environments.

Thanks to the innovations introduced by this collaboration between NASA and Black & Decker, other tools were created for use on Earth – for use in the construction and medical industries, as well as in our homes. The Dustbuster – a light, cordless, hand-held vacuum cleaner – was invented after the Apollo missions, using the technology Black & Decker had developed for NASA. So next time your dad uses one to clean up your mess, remember: it's all thanks to the Moon landings!

MEET THE SCIENTIST

Alonzo Decker Junior was an engineer born in 1908. He graduated from Cornell University with a degree in electrical engineering, and is famous for inventing the cordless electric drill. He was the son of Alonzo G. Decker, founder of Black & Decker.

Speakers

I am sure you have listened to music through a speaker system, or visited a cinema where the sound is loud but crystal-clear. We use speakers so much in our everyday lives that we take them for granted, but some of the technology that makes speakers as good as they are today was developed for the space industry for a completely different purpose.

Why are speakers so good because of space?

In the 1960s, NASA scientists were developing new ideas for ways to get fuel into an engine when it is in a microgravity environment. Normally fuel would flow downwards because of gravity, but in

the absence of gravity the fuel won't flow at all. So a scientist came up with a very clever idea: make the fuel magnetic, then use magnetic fields to attract the fuel up into the engine. This was achieved by adding tiny particles of iron oxide to the fuel.

However, soon after this "ferrofluid" or magnetized fluid was created, rocket-fuel technology changed, and ferrofluids were used to control the temperature of a spacecraft, rather than to move its fuel. A different solution was then found for temperature regulation, and ferrofluids were once again put on the shelf.

However, two scientists involved in the research, Ronald Moskowitz and Ronald E. Rosensweig, realised that while ferrofluids were not going to be utilised for their initial purpose, they could be extremely handy in the future. They formed a company called Ferrofluidics Corporation in the 1960s, and used ferrofluids in various ways over the years – from improving loudspeaker sound quality to controlling vapours escaping into the air during petrol refining.

In 2012, Sony launched a new line of slim speakers, which produce crisper, louder sound in comparison to other speakers of a similar size – and the secret ingredient is the use of the ferrofluid.

Traditional speakers work by translating electrical signals into sounds that our ears can hear. They contain an electromagnet, which is activated when an electric current flows through a wire coil. The electromagnet in the speaker is made to pulse back and forth, creating vibrations in the air that we interpret as sound waves. These waves are amplified (made bigger) by a cone inside the speaker, so that the sound waves are loud enough for us to hear. The vibrations can be made to move quickly or slowly: this affects the type of sound we hear. If you listen to music loud enough, you might be able to see the cones in the speakers vibrating…

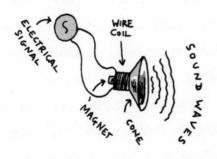

To prevent the cone from moving the wrong way and the coil from wobbling, which could cause the sound to come out incorrectly, the cone in the speaker has a "damper" on it. The damper is usually a ring of material made from almost anything, from cardboard to silk. The damper itself, however, can cause extra vibrations, which make the sound coming from the speaker "fuzzy" and limit its volume.

That's why Sony came up with the idea of using ferrofluid in their speakers instead of a solid damper. A layer of ferrofluid is really thin – much thinner than a piece of cardboard – and this, combined with the way the ferrofluid works with the magnets in the speaker, ensures that there is a lot less friction in the system. Less friction means less energy is wasted, which results in the speaker producing louder, clearer sounds.

So, thanks to the space technology of a magnetised fluid, the speakers in our cinemas, our concert venues and our TVs at home are much better than they used to be. On top of that, because the ferrofluid provides such a thin damper, the speakers can now be built a lot flatter than they were, which means you can have top-of-the-range, attractive speakers in smaller spaces. Thanks, NASA!

AMAZING FACT

Ferrofluids look like pools of oil, but if you bring a magnet close to a ferrofluid, it will go all spiky like a hedgehog!

MEET THE SCIENTIST

The original inventor of ferrofluids was Steve Papell. Papell was born and raised in New York City and was a First Lieutenant in the Army Air Corps during the Second World War. After the war, he gained a degree in mechanical engineering, then worked for NASA for thirty-seven years, which was when he invented ferrofluids. He was ninety-seven when he died in 2015.

Solar Panels

Have you ever wondered why your calculator never needs a new battery? This is probably because it is solar-powered. Solar panels on your calculator convert sunlight, as well as natural and artificial light, into electricity. Solar energy is green, clean and cheap! But did you realise that every time you're punching the keys of your calculator you're using a piece of technology that was developed for use in space?

Why was solar power developed for space?

Scientists were already aware that the sun could be used to make energy way back in the 1800s, and in 1881 a scientist called Charles Fritts created what is believed to be the first ever solar panel. It was extremely inefficient in comparison to coal-burning power plants in making energy, so it didn't really take off. Then, in 1939, a scientist called Russell Ohl built a solar cell that was more efficient, and his design is still used today. The Bell Labs commercialised the solar panel in 1954, and in 1958 Vanguard 1, the first spacecraft to be powered by solar panels, was successfully launched into orbit.

Solar panels are very important in the space industry. Satellites can't be launched with several years' worth of fuel in their tanks, because it would be too heavy and too expensive. Solar panels allow electricity to be created in space, meaning that the spacecraft only needs to carry enough fuel to launch. Once it is in orbit, the satellite can deploy its array of solar panels and start to make energy. The only spacecraft that can't use solar power are the ones that travel too far from the Sun. For example, the Cassini spacecraft, which went to Saturn, where the sun's rays are not strong enough for the solar panels to work, used nuclear power instead. Nowadays, many spacecraft are equipped with solar panels, as are the International Space Station and the Mars rovers. The space industry relies heavily on solar power.

However, despite being adopted by the space industry since the late 1950s, it took some time before solar panels were used to power things on Earth. Luckily, in the 1970s NASA was still paying companies for solar panels to be created, and over the years the space agency has hired many scientists to make them more efficient, better and cheaper than before. This has led to the use of solar power in many everyday objects – from calculators to fridges, heating systems and low-energy lighting appliances.

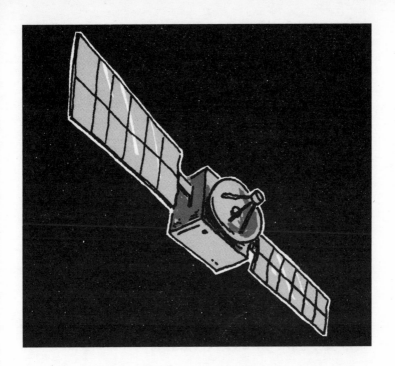

NASA also worked with a company called MicroLink Devices, Inc. in order to improve the efficiency of solar panels and make them thinner. This is a particularly useful measure, because it cuts down on the weight of the solar panels, meaning that launches are cheaper and the overall weight of the spacecraft is lower.

AMAZING FACT

Solar-panel technology is now so advanced you can get a solar panel which is so thin you can roll it up and put it in your pocket!

Such ultra-thin solar panels have been very useful in the military, as soldiers can take flexible, lightweight solar panels with them when they are working in the desert. This means that they don't have to take spare batteries or chargers with them. The solar panels create a source of renewable, portable energy, and the panel can be attached onto a backpack for exposure to sunlight.

The rollable solar panels can be utilised in a variety of ways, from solar tents to solar-powered radio headsets.

MEET THE SCIENTIST

Hans K. Ziegler was a pioneer in the use of solar panels in the space industry. He was born in 1911 in Munich, Germany, where he studied and taught science and engineering before moving to America in 1947. His work was very influential, and the above-mentioned Vanguard 1 was the first-ever spacecraft to be solar-powered, thanks to Hans Ziegler.

HEALTH

Baby Blankets

Sometimes babies are born a little too early. These premature babies are often too small and have trouble maintaining the right body temperature. Special blankets can take care of this problem, which means that they can sleep better – and therefore grow stronger and be less likely to be ill.

These blankets are particularly useful in countries like India, where babies don't always have access  to medical care. Sometimes, being at the right temperature is so important for a baby that they might die if they're not.

Did you know that without the space industry we wouldn't have these blankets? The technology used in them was first designed for astronaut space suits!

Astronauts have to be able to adjust and regulate their temperatures in the extreme conditions of space. A spacesuit has many layers – some for insulation, some to protect an astronaut from radiation and some to absorb sweat, so that astronauts don't get uncomfortable when they wear their suits for long periods of time.

Research into materials for spacesuits started a few decades ago, with the first humans in space, and in the 1980s NASA's Johnson Space Center funded lots of experiments looking into the best fabrics. This research was then taken up by a commercial company, who created "Outlast" – a special fabric that is able to hold heat and transfer it quickly to the right places. Outlast is also non-toxic (it won't harm your skin) and non-flammable (it won't catch fire).

This fabric can be used in sleeping bags, pyjamas and underwear, but recently it has had a more important use. In 2007, Stanford University student Jane Chen and her classmates were tasked with coming up with a way to help look after premature babies. Having only a small budget at their disposal, her team came up with a low-cost design for baby blankets using Outlast. The blankets work by absorbing or releasing heat to keep babies at the right temperature. Jane co-founded a company called Embrace to produce these blankets, which have saved the lives of thousands of babies all over the world.

MEET THE SCIENTIST

Jane Chen lives in San Francisco, California. She has a BA in Psychology and Economics from Pomona College, a Masters in Public Administration from Harvard University and an MBA from Stanford University. In 2013, Jane and the other co-founders of Embrace were awarded the prestigious Economist Innovation Award.

Baby Food

Have you ever been caught red-handed with your fingers in a jar of baby food? Have you ever, while camping, made a meal from a packet by adding hot water? How about dog food? I hope you haven't tried the last one – but if you've tasted any of the above, you've eaten food that was initially developed for the space industry.

Many babies are breastfed when they are small, but sometimes their mothers are not able to do this, or choose not to. So many babies drink powdered formula – milk that has been created artificially, instead of coming from a woman or a cow. The formula is dry, and you add hot water to it to make milk. Without it, many babies can't get the nutrition they need to grow bigger and stronger.

Many years ago, powdered formula milk wasn't as nutritious as breast milk, because it was lacking a substance called omega-3 fatty acids. Too much fat in your food can be harmful for you, but some fats and fatty acids help your body grow properly, and omega-3 is really important in helping babies develop healthy eyes, brains and hearts.

How did the space industry improve formula milk?

In the 1980s, NASA was thinking ahead to a human mission to Mars. In order to send people to Mars, space agencies have to worry about the rockets,

the spacecraft and the cargo – not to mention working out how to keep the crew healthy and safe during their journey and after they arrive. This involves making sure the "Marsonauts" have the correct nutrition available to them. However, it isn't possible to take fruit and vegetables all the way to Mars: the journey takes so long that the food would go mouldy. For that reason, NASA had to start developing different ways to enhance the nutritional quality of food available, so that astronauts would survive long trips in space. NASA did lots of experiments on food, and eventually began working with a company that made one of the most successful "space on Earth" inventions ever.

This company was the Martin Marietta Corporation. They conducted a number of experiments with microalgae – a tiny type of plant that gets its energy from the sun and can turn light into food in a process called photosynthesis. As they were trying to find new ways of making food for astronauts, the scientists at the Martin Marietta Corporation found that microalgae were able to produce the special omega-3. The microalgae was then used to enhance food, including baby food and baby-milk formula, to help people on Earth just as much as the astronauts in space.

This discovery was so exciting that the scientists were able to launch their own company, Martek Biosciences Corporation, in 1985. Martek has since become a huge company, which creates the fatty acids that, in addition to other supplements, make formula milk more nutritious. The products manufactured by Martek can now be found all over the world.

AMAZING FACT

We are able to get omega-3 from certain fish or fish oils. However, the fish don't produce omega-3 themselves: in fact, it is the microalgae they eat that produce these fatty acids, which then enter their bodies!

MEET THE SCIENTISTS

In 1985, the Martin Marietta Corporation decided to shut down the bioscience department that produced the microalgae, so scientists Dr Richard J. Radmer, Dr David Kyle and Dr Paul Behrens opened their own company, Martek, to continue their activities. Dr Richard J. Radmer holds a doctorate in biology from Harvard University and was an associate professor at the University of Maryland before setting up Martek with his colleagues.

Artificial Limbs

People who have suffered amputations – where a leg or arm has to be removed due to disease or an accident – often wear prosthetic (artificial) limbs to help them do things, from day-to-day tasks to competing in international sporting events, as can be seen by the inspirational achievements of athletes during the Paralympic Games.

Prosthetics were first used in ancient Egypt. The big toe might seem like a small part of the body, but it is useful for balance and for pushing the rest of the body forward. Without a big toe it is very difficult to walk – and the ancient Egyptians realised this and made artificial toes from wood and leather to aid those who had lost them.

A fake leg made of bronze was found in a tomb in Italy in 300 BC, showing that prosthetic limbs existed in Roman times. Victorians made artificial hands from metal. In the twenty-first century prosthetics are made from various materials, such as plastic and carbon fibre.

Did you know that the space industry has contributed to the design and creation of prosthetic limbs?

If it wasn't for the space industry, artificial hands and legs wouldn't be as good as they are today. The infamous pirate Long John Silver could have done with a better fake leg!

NASA collaborated with a company called Environmental Robots in order to create robotic arms that can do the work of humans when in space. Some are able to fix parts of the spacecraft and others aid astronauts in their day-to-day activities. They are ideal in a dangerous situation in space, particularly during a long mission to Mars or beyond. By working with Environmental Robots, NASA has contributed to improving the shock absorption, motion capabilities, robotics and comfort of prosthetic limbs. This in turn has helped the advancement of artificial-limb capabilities for human use. Thanks to the space industry, prosthetics now have muscle systems and robotic sensing – which give artificial limbs the ability to move by themselves!

In addition to these enhancements, thanks to NASA's memory-foam technology, prosthetic and robotic limbs have been made to look and feel more like natural human flesh. This special foam also makes prosthetic limbs more comfortable to wear, because it creates a barrier between the skin and the artificial limb, which prevents friction and rubbing, and stops heat or moisture from building up. For the next generation of astronauts, futuristic prosthetics might even be 3D-printed on Mars!

The scientists and engineers at Environmental Robots were so clever that they were able to create muscle systems for robotic arms – even ones with fingers that can hold small objects and pick up delicate items, such as space rocks. These robots are also able to work in the cold darkness of space! The same technology can be used in industrial robots on Earth, and for all types of applications – from toys to smart structures. So if it wasn't for the space industry, prosthetic arms and legs on Earth wouldn't be so advanced, and perhaps everyone would still be wearing artificial limbs made from metal or wood...

AMAZING FACT

Many animals have been given prosthetics to make their lives better. The many notable success stories include an elephant which was fitted with a fake leg after losing one to a landmine, a loggerhead turtle who was given prosthetic flippers after having a run-in with a shark, and an eagle who got a 3D-printed beak to help it eat and drink.

MEET THE SCIENTISTS

Dr Kwang J. Kim is Professor of Energy and Matter at the University of Nevada. He graduated from Yonsei University in South Korea, got his PhD from Arizona State University in America and did research at the University of Maryland, College Park. He has worked for various companies, including a role as Chief Scientist at Environmental Robots.

Dr Mohsen Shahinpoor is a professor of mechanical engineering with a PhD in mechanical and aerospace engineering from the University of Delaware. He has experience in bio-materials and robotic systems engineering and design. He has worked for the Artificial Muscle Research Institute and the Department of Neurosurgery at the UNM Hospital in Albuquerque and is currently at the University of Maine. In 2003 his team were awarded the NASA Space Act Award for their work on artificial muscles.

Cochlear Implants

You may know about hearing aids, which are designed to help people who are hearing-impaired have a better quality of life. But did you know about cochlear implants?

A hearing aid makes sounds louder, but a cochlear implant connects the small bones in your ears to the relevant parts of your brain, effectively doing the job of your ear. When sound waves travel into your ear, the eardrum passes these vibrations to small bones, which transfer them to the cochlea in the inner ear, where they are turned into electrical impulses and travel to the brain, becoming the sounds you hear. For some people, this process is defective, and the cochlear implant can measure the sounds coming through a person's ear and turn them into the electrical signals for the brain to translate, thus replacing the function of the cochlea.

How do cochlear implants relate to space?

In the 1970s, a hearing-impaired electrical engineer working for NASA, Adam Kissiah, spent his lunch breaks and evenings in Kennedy Space Center's library trying to work out how he could improve his hearing. Traditional hearing aids didn't work properly for him, so he tried to design a surgically implantable device to provide hearing sensations for the hearing-impaired.

For three years, Kissiah devoted his spare time to designing the cochlear implant, outside his working hours for NASA. The incredible thing is that he had no specific medical expertise, but drew on the knowledge of electrical engineering he had amassed while he was working for NASA in the Space Shuttle programme, which included creating sound, electronic and vibration sensors. Using these skills, he created an early form of the cochlear implant, which relied on electrical signal processing instead of amplification of sound.

It just goes to show that the everyday-life applications for space-industry research are infinite, and can help people in unforeseen ways!

AMAZING FACT

There are over a quarter of a million users of cochlear implants in the world, of which more than ten thousand are in the UK – so we should all feel confident and grateful for hearing technology and its ability to transform lives!

MEET THE SCIENTIST

Adam Kissiah was born in Charlotte, North Carolina, and graduated from Oakhurst High School in May 1947. After four years in the Navy, he joined NASA in 1963, where he worked for twenty-six years. He had many roles at NASA, from launch-instrumentation-systems engineer and staff engineer to technical manager. He supported many of the human-spaceflight and shuttle programmes, including Mercury, Gemini, Apollo, Apollo Skylab and Apollo-Soyuz. He won many awards for his inventions.

Cancer Detectors

Sadly, many people still suffer from cancer. One way of giving cancer patients a longer and happier life – if not curing them altogether – is to detect the disease early on, so it can be removed before it spreads. There is a special diagnostic tool called BioScan which can confirm the presence of cancer in a tissue at the very earliest stages by looking for tiny changes in temperature.

Digital sensors like BioScan detect something called infrared waves, which are part of the electromagnetic spectrum, like visible light, microwaves and X-rays. Most heat produces infrared radiation. The technology in the BioScan that finds the infrared waves is called the "quantum well infrared photodetector" (QWIP). QWIP can detect infrared energy coming from specific parts of the body, such as cancerous tissues that can emit heat. Using QWIP to diagnose cancer is pain-free as well, unlike other methods: it feels just like having your photograph taken.

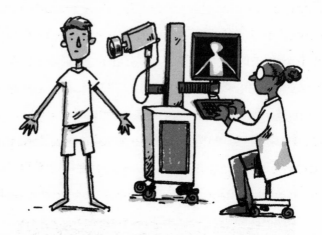

AMAZING FACT

Since it can detect heat energy, or infrared waves, in the same way that the human eye can see visible light, QWIP is also used to identify forest fires and investigate volcanic activity.

Did you know that the detectors using QWIP technology were originally designed by scientists at NASA to discover planets in space?

Charge-coupled devices, or CCDs – already mentioned in the 'Technology' section – are tiny chips that can convert light into digital images. NASA has created many types of CCDs for space missions, including extremely sensitive ones allowing the Hubble Space Telescope to take excellent pictures of the universe. The same type of CCD that is used for taking space pictures can now also be

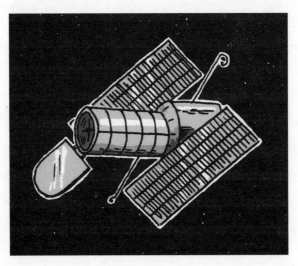

utilised to detect cancer cells, because the CCDs are able to find the tiniest details.

Older techniques to diagnose cancer included biopsies (removing a small sample of body tissue). This would involve surgery to remove part of the tissue in order to test it. The CCDs are part of a miniscule digital camera with X-ray vision that can look for and detect cancerous tissue. Doctors are able to inject the CCD cameras into the patient, which means that patients don't have to undergo surgery, and they are left with a small puncture instead of a large cut that would need stitches. And as well as avoiding unnecessary pain and trauma, the CCD procedure is cheaper than surgery.

AMAZING FACT

Each time a biopsy was done it would cost tens of thousands of pounds. With the new method using CCDs it costs about £850 each time! This is saving health services around the world billions of pounds per year!

MEET THE SCIENTIST

Carolyn Krebs worked for NASA for twenty years, and before that she was at the University of Missouri and McDonnell Douglas Astronautics Company. During her time at NASA's Goddard Space Flight Center, she was the Project Instrument Detector Lead for the Advanced Camera for Surveys and the Instrument Manager for the  Space Telescope Imaging Spectrograph (STIS) on the Hubble Space Telescope. The CCDs that were part of the STIS were developed by Carolyn Krebs and her team and went on to be used to diagnose cancer. Along with other scientists and engineers who worked on these CCDs, she was inducted into the Space Technology Hall of Fame in 1997 for her work on CCDs and cancer detection.

Helping Those with Dementia

As you get older, the way your brain works starts to change. Dementia is a general term for many conditions that can have an impact on your brain, from memory loss to Alzheimer's disease. Most of these are due to old age, but sometimes dementia can affect younger people. Some of the symptoms of dementia-driven illnesses are forgetfulness, inability to focus or concentrate and impaired communication and language.

Perhaps you know someone with dementia already – maybe a grandparent or a great-grandparent. People who have dementia might face smaller problems like forgetting where they left their keys or putting something in the wrong place, but their condition can also manifest itself in more dangerous forms, such as leaving a frying pan on the hob or walking aimlessly in the street. All forms of dementia can be very sad, both for the affected person and their friends and family.

Did you know the space industry has helped dementia patients, and may help more in the future?

NASA and the space industry regularly examine astronauts while they are in space to investigate the effects of space travel on the human body. Many of the conditions that astronauts suffer from in space are similar to those that afflict the elderly on Earth, from osteoporosis to sight problems.

Space dementia can occur when astronauts spend too long in space, since their constant exposure to radiation can cause brain damage. Astronauts on the International Space Station are safer, as they are close enough to Earth to be protected from the radiation by the Earth's magnetic field, but astronauts travelling

for years in space could suffer from memory impairments, reduced body functions, loss of awareness and long-term brain conditions. Because of this, space agencies are investigating the causes of dementia and potential cures, and this research benefits those on Earth who are already afflicted by it.

In addition to the research on dementia undertaken by the space industry, some other scientific advances have helped in the fight against this condition. Dr Norden Huang has developed a new diagnostic method that can detect damage to spacecraft by analysing changes in their signals. This technology, called the Hilbert-Huang Transform (HHT), can also be used in other industries – from creating better submarines and reducing the noise from motorways to helping both the finance and medical professions. A bio-medical company, DynaDx Corporation, used HHT to monitor brain blood flow and detect irregularities that can cause dementia.

Blood moves around the brain to various sections, depending on what you are doing and where it is required. If a person is suffering from dementia or other brain-related conditions, the blood flow to the brain is altered. If this change is detected quickly, the damage to the brain can be limited. All thanks to a technology first designed for the space shuttle...

Another example of space technology that has been adapted for the National Health Service in the UK is patient-tracking slippers.

GPS chips are placed in the soles of comfortable shoes, which people with dementia are urged to wear. This GPS footwear, also known as SmartSoles, can alert a medical professional or carer via an app over the Internet if someone with dementia gets lost or wanders too far from home. The wearer can be found quickly and safely. And if you are able to track dementia patients, you can give them more independence to go out and about alone, which means fewer worries for their carers, as well as fewer hospital visits for the patients. Not bad for a small GPS chip – first created for the space industry – and a pair of slippers!

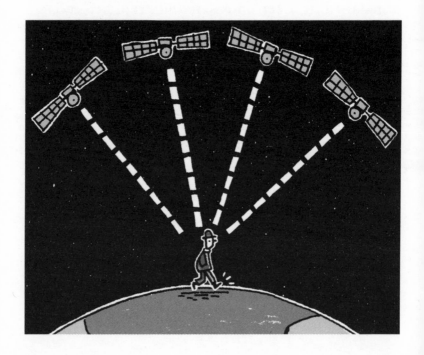

AMAZING FACT

If you have ever worn a smartwatch or fitness tracker, you are wearing something very similar to the patient-tracking slippers, as these devices also contain a GPS chip to monitor your location.

MEET THE SCIENTIST

Dr Norden Huang has a PhD in Fluid Mechanics and Mathematics from Johns Hopkins University. During his time at NASA's Goddard Space Flight Center, he used his mathematical skills to study how ocean waves are affected by wind and water currents. For his HHT invention, he was awarded the 1998, 2003 and 2004 NASA Special Space Act Awards.

FASHION

UV-Blocking Sunglasses

Sunglasses are dark glasses with special filters on the lenses designed to protect your eyes from being hurt or damaged by the bright ultraviolet (UV) light from the sun and other sources. As well as being able to block out harmful UV rays, sunglasses enhance vision in bright conditions. You might have worn a pair to ward off the sun's rays or, if you've been skiing, to stop your eyes being blinded by the sunlight reflecting off the snow.

As UV light enters the eye, it can affect our ability to see clearly. This is because light travels through the pupil and reaches the retina, a type of projector screen on the back of the eye. The retina contains rod- and cone-shaped photoreceptors – rods help

us to see black and white in low light and cones are used for colour vision and tiny details. There are hundreds of millions of rods and cones in a human eye. Harmful UV light can damage the rods and cones, causing visual impairment and sometimes blindness, so it is very important to block it out.

How do sunglasses relate to space? Do astronauts wear sunglasses?

Scientists Charles Miller and James Stephens worked at NASA's Jet Propulsion Laboratory in the 1980s. There they were studying the effects of harmful radiation from space and UV rays and their effect on the human body – especially the eyes.

In order to protect our eyes from this sort of radiation, the two scientists designed materials capable of absorbing and filtering the danger-ous light, based on their observations of birds of prey. As these birds require excellent vision in order to hunt their prey in all weather condi-tions, their eyes form a protective layer of oil that filters out harmful radiation, allowing them to see particular wavelengths of visible light in complete safety. The clever thing is that the oil not only protects the birds' eyes, but also enhances their vision, meaning that they can hunt smaller

prey from greater distances. The NASA scientists replicated this idea for protective goggles with a substance called zinc oxide instead of oil as the filter.

The NASA-inspired sunglasses, aptly named "Eagle Eyes", permit safe and clear viewing, because they block out the UV rays and stop too much blue light coming in, allowing at the same time the visible light to enter the eye.

These inventions helped enhance the fashionable UV-blocking sunglasses we all know and wear today. And these sunglasses aren't just a fashion item: the spin-off company that make the NASA-inspired specs donate glasses to children at risk of cataracts, such as those who live in Alaska, where the sun's rays are more dangerous, because they are reflected off the snow. However, these glasses can't make you have the eyes of an eagle!

AMAZING FACT

You may think that darker sunglasses are better, but that isn't always the case. The darker sunglasses do filter out the harmful rays, but they also relax your eye, which allows more blue light to reach its rod and cone photosensors. And too much blue light can be dangerous.

Skiwear

Everyone loves a snowball fight when the weather gets a bit colder… and some people also enjoy skiing and other winter sports. Skiwear has changed over the years and has given rise to ski fashion, serving the purpose of keeping you warm, but also allowing you to pose on the slopes as if it were a catwalk! And thanks to innovations in skiwear today, winter sports are safer than ever before.

Did you know that without the space industry skiing wouldn't be the same?

When you are skiing, of course, the actual skis are important, but so is the rest of the gear, such as boots, glasses and outerwear.

The boots connect the skis to your body, so they play a crucial role in your performance. If you have bad boots, the best skis in the world won't help you. Ski boots were originally normal boots tied to skis, but they evolved into very tough ones made from rigid material. Skiers, however, found these uncomfortable, and often ended up with sore or bruised legs.

A product developer called Erik Giese realised that he could improve boots by incorporating a corrugated

(bendable like an accordion or a drinking straw) design into them. The original idea for this had been devised by NASA to make it easier for astronauts to move their joints when they were in a spacesuit. The corrugated design in a ski boot gives your foot more flexibility at the ankle and allows you to move it forwards and backwards more freely, while still giving you good ankle support.

Erik Giese founded a company in the 1970s called Comfort Products, which produced this new type of ski boot in collaboration with other shoe manufacturers. The boots came out in the 1980s and were the first ski footwear with hinged ankles. This prevented skiers from having as many accidents, and Olympic athletes quickly adopted the boots.

Astronaut Gene Cernan, the last man to walk on the Moon, found that his goggles kept misting up when he was in space, so he couldn't do his job properly. Back in the laboratories, scientists created a de-fogger made from liquid soap, oil and water, which was later used on the Eagle Eyes sunglasses. This de-fogger is also sold to companies who make goggles for skiers, as well as equipment for deep-sea divers and cars.

Since astronauts have to be able to stand extreme conditions in space, they must wear protective clothing. The same goes for skiers, who need to be kept warm and protected from accidents when skiing. NASA worked with a company called Aspen Systems to create an insulating material to be used in space. Aspen Systems came up with the idea of using an aerogel to meet the needs of the astronauts.

Aerogels were invented a long time before humans went to space. They are made by producing a gel and replacing its liquid part with a gas. This makes aerogels extremely light: they are, essentially, like a high-tech sponge.

In 1993, NASA worked with Aspen Systems to create aerogels using new techniques which made them stronger, more flexible and more insulating than before, so that they could be used in all types of situations. Aspen Systems called this aerogel Spaceloft, and in 2001 Corpo Nove produced a jacket which had Spaceloft in it, with wonderful heat-retaining properties, which has enhanced the experience of skiers all over the world.

Similar scientific developments were also applied to ski gloves. So thanks to the space industry, you can keep warm, see clearly and be more stable on your skis when you go skiing.

MEET THE SCIENTIST

Erik Giese was born in Seattle, USA, and skied at a high level when he was at the University of Washington. After getting a law degree at the University of Washington, he practised law in Seattle. In 1973 he founded Comfort Products, which produced the first commercially viable flexible ski boot. Through his companies, he collaborated with NASA, Ford and the US military. He passed away in 2016.

Swimsuits

When you go on holiday, or just down to the local swimming pool for a dip, I am sure you remember to take the essentials. Towel, tick. Goggles, tick. Rubber ring, tick! Swimming costume, tick! It would make swimming in public a bit more awkward if you had to wear a nineteenth-century-style swimsuit...

Swimming costumes have changed over the years in size, material, comfort and efficiency. Olympic swimmers have to decide carefully what to wear, as the wrong swimsuit could cost them a gold medal.

Swimming-costume design really took off in the Victorian times, when swimming for pleasure became fashionable. Ladies would wear a full-length gown, a bit like a dressing gown, often

made from wool or flannel. As you can imagine, these would get very heavy when wet, but people believed they would keep you warm if you went swimming in the cold sea. Over time, the material used for swimsuits changed from wool and flannel to Rayon – an artificially produced material – jersey and silk, and eventually to latex and other synthetic fabrics. After the Second World War, there was a shortage of some of these materials, which resulted in smaller swimming costumes – and bare midriffs!

By the 1950s, swimsuits had evolved even further. Speedo was the first company to include nylon in their products. Racing-style swimwear became popular, and swimmers who took part in competitions were mindful of the material and shape of their swimwear, because this has a knock-on effect on the speed in water. The smaller and smoother the swimwear, the more "streamlined" and fast the swimmer.

Did you know that the space industry has had a part to play in the advancement of swimming-costume designs?

It's not just swimmers that need to be streamlined in order to move more efficiently. Spacecraft and rockets also have to be able to withstand a lot of drag, or air resistance, when they are launched into the air – and the smoother and more streamlined they are, the quicker they can lift off and the less fuel they will use.

NASA inventors at the Langley Research Center were investigating materials and design adjustments that could reduce air resistance. "Riblets" were invented by NASA in the 1980s: they are small grooves on the surface of objects which reduce drag. Riblets were adopted by many other industries, including the sportswear industry, and were used in swimsuits made by a company who supply sports equipment to triathletes. It has been reported that these swimsuits are ten per cent faster than any other in the world!

The ribbing on the Strush SR swimsuit is adapted to enchance the particular stroke a swimmer wants to use. Swimmers who wore the Strush SR swimwear in the 1995 Pan American Games won thirteen gold medals, three silver and one bronze. And that is not the only contribution of the space industry to swimwear.

Space agencies test the aerodynamics of objects in wind tunnels: their scientists and engineers can use the results to improve their designs. Speedo's Aqualab research unit employed NASA wind tunnels to investigate how streamlined their swimsuits were. Different fabrics were evaluated, and, with the help of NASA scientist Stephen Wilkinson, Speedo created the LZR Racer range of swim-wear, made from a fabric called LZR Pulse, which reduces drag, repels water and is very light.

NASA and Speedo also tested different types of seams, which are the main cause of drag. Speedo were able to create a new type of seam, where the pieces of fabric are "ultrasonically bonded", rather than sewn together. In addition to making the swimming costume more aerodynamic, these bonded seams ensure that it is also able to grip the body more tightly, which helps the swimmers per-form for a longer time and faster. In March 2008, athletes wearing the LZR Racer swimsuit broke thirteen world records.

AMAZING FACT

The full-body version of the LZR Racer has been banned from international competitions because it was making swimmers *too* good!

MEET THE SCIENTIST

Stephen Wilkinson has a Bachelor degree in Engineering Science and a Masters in Mechanical Engineering from Old Dominion University. He is an inventor and a research engineer and has worked for the NASA Langley Research Center as an aerospace engineer for forty years.

Braces

I hope you never had to wear "train-track" braces on your teeth – those awful things with wires that make you look like a "metal mouth"... Sure, they did a great job, but train-track braces just don't cut it. (Well, in fact they do cut the inside of your mouth...) This is where invisible braces come in.

They work in the same way as the older braces: wires and brackets connect to the teeth to move them slowly over time, until they are perfectly aligned. But the advantage is that they are barely noticeable, and because they have a slightly different structure, they are not as painful as train tracks. First conceived in the 1980s, invisible braces are now being used widely – even by Hollywood celebrities!

Did you know that invisible braces were first invented for the space industry?

There has always been a link between astronauts and dentists, because early space-travellers used to brush their teeth with "astronaut toothpaste", which sadly isn't produced any more. What made this toothpaste special was that it didn't foam up, and could be swallowed after brushing one's teeth. This was helpful for astronauts, as they didn't have to spit in zero gravity – potentially a very messy affair. However, astronauts now use "normal" toothpaste and spit into a towel.

But invisible braces represent the space industry's biggest contribution to dental care. The first step towards their invention was made by a company called Ceradyne, with the help of NASA. Ceradyne produced ceramic materials for many different industries in the fields of aerospace and electronics. NASA was looking for a new material that could be used for their spacecraft – one that was tougher and stronger than anything currently available – and the scientists at Ceradyne came up with something called transparent polycrystalline alumina (TPA), which, as the name suggests, is see-through, and was originally used to protect the infrared antennae of heat-seeking missile trackers.

A few years later, Unitek Corporation contacted Ceradyne, as they were looking for a material for their new braces. Ceradyne suggested TPA, and this is how the new braces were born.

AMAZING FACT

As TPA is stronger than steel, transparent and smooth, it is also used on the sides and under-carriages of trucks and lorries to protect them.

MEET THE SCIENTIST

Joel Moskowitz was only twenty-eight when he thought about starting his own business. He had a degree in ceramic engineering from Alfred University and spent five years working in ceramics research while working at night towards his MBA degree at the University of Southern California. After getting his degree, his passion for ceramics drove him to start Ceradyne Inc.

Sports Clothes

As I am sure you're aware, there are infinite varieties of sporting equipment available if you do sport – from running tops to breathable T-shirts and hiking jackets – not to mention trainers…

But did you realise that when you do any type of sport, from walking in the mountains to running around a tennis court, you could be wearing technology originally created for the space industry?

As we saw in the 'Skiwear' chapter, there is a special type of insulation that can regulate temperature. It works by storing the heat that is created when something changes phase – from gas to liquid, for example – this is why it's called "phase-changing material" (PCM). The stored heat can then be given off when it is needed, which means the insulation can control temperature. Some PCMs were designed first for the space industry – in order to help astronauts keep cool or warm and comfortable during their long space walks.

It was space-agency engineers who first came up with the idea of liquid-cooling clothing. This was achieved by running small "veins" of water through spacesuits in order to change their temperature whenever it was needed. Over time, however, they started to investigate other methods of producing fabrics that could control temperature without needing to sew water channels into them.

In the 1980s, NASA teamed up with small businesses in a bid to find new phase-changing materials that would meet the needs of their astronauts. Outlast Technologies developed microPCMs called "thermocules" that could be incorporated into textiles. Thermocules react to temperature changes, then release or absorb heat depending on the environment. They can be used in a variety of ways and are safe to use in fabrics near the skin.

Nowadays, Outlast make all types of products containing thermocules – from activewear to winter-sporting wear, from sleeping bags to polo shirts. Their products can be found in large British retailers such as Marks & Spencer, and some of their technology is used by big sports brands like Reebok. So if you have a polo shirt from M&S or Reebok, you might be wearing space technology!

Many running tops use "wicking" technology, which draws sweat away from the body and makes you feel more comfortable when you're doing exercise. It brings the moisture directly to the surface, which means the sweat evaporates more quickly. This technology started at NASA, and was also used for spacesuits and astronauts.

Sports shoes have also had the "space" treatment. Astronauts have to wear big, heavy boots, so engineers have come up with a clever way for making them feel more comfortable: they have created a material that can absorb shock and reduce tiredness in the feet. This is now often used in trainers and in a variety of sports shoes.

This special material and the air chambers under the foot become squashed when the wearer jumps or runs. As the foot continues to move, the fabric springs back upwards, giving more momentum. The use of this space-industry innovation in trainers can therefore reduce injury and help performance.

This technology, which has enhanced sportswear, has also been used to enhance dresswear or smart clothes!

Smart shirts have been created by a company called Ministry of Supply. Two of its founders, Gihan Amarasiriwardena and Kevin Rustagi, met while they were studying chemical and biological engineering at MIT. Gihan used to design water-proof jackets and running clothes when he was a young boy, and Kevin dreamt of innovative clothes that would keep him comfortable and stylish, while their colleague Kit Hickey wanted her office cloth-ing to be as useful as her climbing wear. The three of them met Eddie Obropta Jr, who was also a student at MIT and was working on a human mission to Mars. Through Eddie the team learnt about PCMs and decided to start the Ministry of Supply in order to include PCMs in smart shirts – so anyone can go to a posh dinner and not worry about their shirts showing sweat patches! Their first product, a white dinner shirt with PCMs in it, was named Apollo, after the Moon missions.

MEET THE SCIENTIST

Kit Hickey is an "entrepreneur in residence" at the Martin Trust Center and a lecturer at the MIT Sloane School of Management. She teaches people about starting their own businesses, and she loves mountain sports. Kit, Gihan and Kevin were all athletes who met at MIT before co-founding the Ministry of Supply.

Bike Helmets

Do you know how to ride a bike? Perhaps you're learning? Maybe you had a scooter when you were little, or you play American football? All of these activities have something in common: you wear a helmet to protect your head from injury.

People have been wearing helmets to protect their heads for hundreds of years. Gone, however, are the old metal helmets covering the whole head: nowadays, helmets are made of lighter plastic materials or resin, are reinforced with fibres and are more aerodynamic.

And the space industry has helped the helmet become what we know and use today.

In the 1980s, Jim Gentes, a producer of bike helmets, teamed up with an aerodynamicist at NASA, Raymond Hicks, to make a new helmet using technology which was developed by NASA's predecessor NACA in the Second World War to reduce the drag on fighter planes. They estimated that, thanks to this technology, cyclists could save one second in each kilometre they pedalled.

NASA are also behind the invention of memory foam, which was designed in the 1960s to pad astronauts' seats, reducing discomfort during launch by absorbing shocks.

Charles Yost, an aeronautical engineer, helped to create a recovery system for the Apollo command module between 1962 and 1966. He was then contracted by NASA, and worked with the space agency on various survival systems for astronauts, including creating the memory-foam material that we see in all sorts of products today. Memory foam is now used in mattresses and pillows, protecting bedridden elderly patients from bedsores, as well as in shoes.

Memory foam matches the shape of the body and returns to the original shape once the pressure on it is removed. When an astronaut is sitting in the spacecraft during lift-off, they are subject to additional forces which push them down in their seats. The memory-foam seating helps to protect the astronaut by changing its shape as pressure is applied to it.

AMAZING FACT

Memory foam can return to its original shape even if it is compressed up to ninety per cent. A 7-cm-thick piece of memory foam can absorb all the energy of an adult falling from a height of three metres!

But did you realise that some helmets have memory foam in them as well? By lining the helmet with this material, the wearer is more protected than if they were wearing a plain plastic helmet: the memory foam can adjust to the shape of their head without putting additional pressure on any particular area. The padding made from memory foam, first created by NASA, helps to cushion the wearer's head from knocks, bumps and injuries. Helmets with memory foam can absorb three times the shock than those without it.

MEET THE SCIENTIST

Charles Yost was born in 1933. After getting a degree in aeronautical engineering from Northrop University in 1962, he worked as a research engineer for NASA and was the original developer of memory foam. He loved astronomy, space and physics, and he set up the Sunlight Foundation in 2004 to encourage research in scientific and educational studies, particularly in natural and physical sciences.

Now you've discovered some of the spin-offs available to humans on Earth – technologies that were first developed in the space industry to make astronauts safer or make spacecraft work better. You can see that the space industries across the globe don't just work to enhance the lives of those involved with space travel: these inventions can often help everyday people, sometimes saving lives. Now that you've read about some of the incredible objects on Earth that are from space, perhaps you'll look at your everyday objects in a different light. Perhaps you might investigate, or even create, your own space on Earth!